IMAGES
of America

CINCINNATI PARKS AND PARKWAYS

One of the Queen City's best-known landmarks, Cincinnati Union Terminal looms over a formerly bustling 19th-century neighborhood. This view suggests the great urban density of the city, a major factor driving creation of Cincinnati's public parks. At the time of this 1972 photograph, prospects for both the terminal and the neighborhood were grim. The neighborhood was soon lost to redevelopment, but hard work and a forward-looking citizenry preserved the old railroad station as the Cincinnati Museum Center. Beginning in the early 20th century, a similar progressive vision over many years gave the city an unmatched system of parks and scenic parkways. (Author's collection.)

ON THE COVER: A band concert was a sure way to draw a crowd in the pre-radio, pre-television days of the early 20th century. If it was a warm summer day, and if the setting offered green grass and abundant shade, so much the better. This 1915 view, facing north, shows the Eden Park Music Pavilion during just such an event. Adults and children alike are dressed in their cool summer whites. Note how carefully everyone has avoided standing or sitting in the sun. (Cincinnati Park Board Archives.)

IMAGES
of America

CINCINNATI PARKS AND PARKWAYS

Nancy A. Recchie
and Jeffrey T. Darbee

ARCADIA
PUBLISHING

ISBN 978-0-7385-8394-5

Published by Arcadia Publishing
Charleston, South Carolina

Printed in the United States of America

Library of Congress Control Number: 2010905380

For all general information contact Arcadia Publishing at:
Telephone 843-853-2070
Fax 843-853-0044
E-mail sales@arcadiapublishing.com
For customer service and orders:
Toll-Free 1-888-313-2665

Visit us on the Internet at www.arcadiapublishing.com

Cincinnati's parks have long offered more than just recreational opportunities. These diligent young artists, in their late 50s or early 60s today, get up close to nature as they sculpt bird models with the help of some real-life examples. The Trailside Museum in Burnet Woods, built in 1939 and today called the Trailside Nature Center, has held many such classes over the years. It continues to offer numerous nature programs for children and adults. (Cincinnati Park Board Archives.)

Contents

Acknowledgments

This book grew from a research project on Cincinnati's parks, during which several park board staffers generously gave their time and assistance. Our thanks go to Steven Schuckman, superintendent, Division of Planning and Design, Cincinnati Park Board; Vivian Wagner, Bettman Natural Resource Center; and Vicki Newell, Cincinnati Park Board Library and Archives.

Special thanks to our son James Darbee for enduring yet another round of sorting, scanning, and organizing photographs.

Many sources of information were helpful in preparing the text, although, as is often the case, not all of them agreed about all the factual details. Of particular help was *A Guide to Art and Architecture in Cincinnati's Parks*, published by the City of Cincinnati in 1995.

And, as always, our thanks for help and patience go to Melissa Basilone, our editor at Arcadia Publishing.

Lisa Schafer has been credited for the several photographs she took. Unless otherwise noted, all images are from the Cincinnati Park Board Archives. Photographs by the authors are credited as "Author's collection."

INTRODUCTION

"The location of Cincinnati is one of peculiar natural beauty. The city is principally built on a plateau, through which the (Ohio) river passes . . . This great plain is entirely surrounded by a chain of hills, rising to an altitude of three hundred feet, forming one of the most beautiful natural amphitheaters to be found anywhere on the continent, from whose hilltops may be seen the splendid panorama of the cities below with the winding Ohio . . . (N)o large city of the United States presents such a strikingly picturesque variety of position and scenery."

— History of Cincinnati and Hamilton County

This passage from the 1894 *History of Cincinnati and Hamilton County* illustrates why Cincinnati has often been described as a city within a park. Nature endowed, and early settlers selected, a city site that would prove to be unusually well suited for industrial, commercial, and residential development. In time, it would also lend itself to creation of an outstanding system of public parks that took great advantage of and creatively enhanced the area's natural features.

In 1788, surveyors laid out what would become known as "The Queen City of the West," and the construction of Fort Washington the next year marked the beginning of settlement on the flat land above the north bank of the Ohio River. The place was first called Losantiville, a blend of French and Latin that meant "the town opposite the mouth of the Licking River." After settlement began in earnest following the Treaty of Greenville in 1795, Gen. Arthur St. Clair, governor of the Northwest Territory, changed the little community's name to the more attractive Cincinnati, in honor of the group of Revolutionary War veterans known as the Society of the Cincinnati.

Cincinnati was chartered in 1802, a year before Ohio became the nation's 17th state. The city had a strategic position midway between the beginning of the Ohio River at Pittsburgh and its junction with the Mississippi River at Cairo, Illinois. Cincinnati became the port of entry for a large hinterland that would eventually become part of the states of Ohio, Indiana, and Kentucky.

Over 2,500 people called Cincinnati home by 1810. The next year, the pioneer steamboat *New Orleans* would prove the practicability of steam-powered river navigation, and within the next seven years, some 80 steamboats traveled the Ohio and other western rivers, a quarter of them having been built in Cincinnati. The early flatboats and keelboats that had dominated river travel for almost a century rapidly disappeared.

Development in the city, at first, was confined to the flat riverside land known as "the Basin." Until population pressures created demand for more land, and technological developments such as streetcars and inclines made it feasible, development in the hills surrounding the Basin proceeded only slowly.

Just as the steamboat had revolutionized river travel (Cincinnati would see some 8,000 annual steamboat arrivals and departures by mid-century), changes in the technology of land transportation enhanced commerce and communication across Ohio, with direct benefits for Cincinnati.

Unpaved pioneer roads and trails, more a hindrance than a spur to development, first gave way to the state-supported system of canals. The Miami and Erie Canal, one of two cross-state routes, connected the Queen City with Dayton by 1829. By the 1850s, the canal had reached Toledo, giving some of the state's most fertile agricultural land a reliable outlet to widespread markets via both Lake Erie and the Ohio River. Commerce flowing through Cincinnati increased greatly as a result.

However, inherent disadvantages of canal transportation, primarily its slow speed and the annual winter shutdown, made it vulnerable to the next transportation revolution: the railroad. Cincinnati's pioneer line, the Little Miami Railroad, connected the city with Xenia by 1845, Columbus by 1850, and Cleveland by 1851. Between 1851 and 1860, construction of other routes into and out of the Queen City had firmly linked it to the nation's fast-growing network of trunk line railroads.

Reliable rail transportation meant rapid industrial growth, and Cincinnati's distinctive topography strongly influenced where this would occur. The valley of Mill Creek, west of the downtown area, offered the right combination of location and resources, along with the area known as the Norwood Trough. Laced with rail lines and home to such well-known manufacturers as Procter and Gamble and the United States Playing Card Company, the city's growing industrial base offered employment to uncounted thousands of newly-arrived people, many of them foreign immigrants. They settled in densely built neighborhoods such as Over-the-Rhine (named for its German population and its separation from the downtown area by the canal) and in other districts where residential and commercial development began to spread outward and upward into the hillsides.

All these hardworking people wanted opportunities for rest and relaxation, driven in no small part by the need for green and shady places to escape the summer heat. Especially among citizens of German heritage, beer gardens were popular, but they were not particularly suited as places for wholesome family entertainment. Over time, the need for public parks became more and more obvious.

Development of Cincinnati's parks and parkways did not happen by accident. From early park development before 1820 through development of the pivotal 1907 plan that set the future course and character of the city's parks, Cincinnatians recognized the potential benefits of blending nature with art and architecture. During the 20th century, park designer George Kessler's brilliant 1907 plan, which provided a vision and captured the imagination of the community, set the standard for ongoing park development.

Modern Cincinnati benefits from an extensive public park system totaling more than 5,000 acres (almost 8 square miles), with a series of parkways that provide easy connections among various parts of the city. Parks range from small neighborhood green spaces to large regional parks with historic buildings, extensive planned landscapes, and dramatic vistas of the city and the great valley of the Ohio River. With the recent restoration of many important park buildings, pavilions, and overlooks, Cincinnati has readied its park system for another successful century of serving all of the Queen City's citizens and its millions of annual visitors.

Cincinnati's park system today reflects the visionary leadership of city officials, community leaders, and an active park board; the imprint of talented architects and landscape architects who have shaped the system over a period of nearly two centuries; and the stewardship of a community that long ago made the commitment to step forward with the resources needed to develop and maintain an outstanding collection of parks that welcome all who care to enjoy them.

One

Cincinnati's Early Parks

Until the 1870s, Cincinnati had few public parks. There was no overall park plan or design scheme, and by about 1850, only 20 acres of parks served the city's burgeoning population. At that time, Cincinnati had 115,435 citizens, and by 1870 that figure was 216,239, an increase of 87 percent. Most people were working class and lived on densely developed streets with few opportunities for recreation or relief from the often oppressive summer heat.

The land that became Cincinnati's first park was originally intended as the site of a public market house. Brothers John and Benjamin Piatt donated a long, narrow plot, under an acre in size, in 1817. The market never was built, and the land remained open space until it was developed and dedicated as a park in 1868. Still known as Piatt Park, it remains an important green space in downtown Cincinnati.

There were three other early parks. Washington Park, the "front yard" of the Cincinnati Music Hall in the Over-the-Rhine neighborhood, is 5.5 acres in size and began as a cemetery. Land acquisition by the city was completed in 1863, followed by construction of the Cincinnati Music Hall across Elm Street in 1878. In 1888, several buildings of the Centennial Exposition of the Ohio Valley and Central States were located here, and for many years the park was heavily used by the surrounding neighborhood.

Hopkins Park, a small park on Mount Auburn, was donated by a successful merchant and land developer specifically for a public park. The donor required that the park should "forever be kept free of buildings, and . . . should be tastefully laid out and planted with trees and shrubbery."

The land in Lincoln Park was acquired from Cincinnati Township between 1834 and 1837. Originally there was a cemetery and orphanage on the site, but after 1858, development of the park went forward. It provided West End residents with a public green, walkways, a lake, and landscaping. In 1933, Lincoln Park became the grand entrance for the new Cincinnati Union Terminal. The park has since been removed, and its site is today occupied by large parking lots and roadways.

These early parks were welcomed by the city's residents, but much more needed to be done. Fortunately it was not long before public-minded citizens and a talented landscape designer began to shape the ideas that would spur the growth of an unmatched legacy of great public parks.

About 1800 this was the view if a flatboat passenger were to look toward the north bank of the Ohio River at Cincinnati. Modest settlement had occurred mainly on the Ohio's floodplain and had not yet extended beyond the bluff upon which most of the city's urban core was later built. The artist has suggested the busy river traffic that would be so important to the life and commerce of Cincinnati later in the century. Beyond the bluff, abundant flat land beckoned developers and city

builders, while the tree-bedecked hills would prove to be ideal locations for residential, institutional, and park development. Well-known streets had already been laid out. Main Street cuts through the bluff where a flatboat has moored. To its west is Walnut and Sycamore Streets and Broadway are to the east. Fort Washington, which stood until 1808, is in the distance at right center.

This upriver view from Mount Echo Park, made in the early 20th century, shows the broad sweep of the Ohio River and the hills along both of its banks. Downtown Cincinnati is at left center, and in front of it is the massive steel bridge of the Southern Railway, which was known as the "Queen and Crescent Route," because it connected the Queen (Cincinnati) and Crescent (New Orleans) cities. Ludlow, Kentucky, is on the sloping riverside land on the right side of the photograph. The view looks almost straight east from Mount Echo Park from an elevation of over 800 feet above sea level. In the foreground, some 300 feet below, commercial buildings line River Road, while along the river are railroad tracks leading to St. Louis and Chicago. In this period, steamboat wharves, railroads, and industrial properties lined most of the Ohio's banks, with little access to the river for recreational purposes.

One of Cincinnati's oldest parks did not begin as a park. Memorial Pioneer Cemetery, located along Wilmer Avenue, is sandwiched between Eastern Avenue and the former Lunken Field on the western floodplain of the Little Miami River. This photograph, taken in 1915, shows the poor condition of the cemetery at the time. Today it is part of the city's park system, and it is carefully tended in recognition of its importance as the final resting place of many early settlers. The view looks southwest toward the Ohio River; to the right is the curving track of the Little Miami Railroad's line to its downtown Cincinnati terminal at Court Street. The cemetery is located well outside today's city core because the pioneer settlement of Columbia was in this area. Out of view to the right is the 300-foot-high hill atop which Alms Park was established after land was donated to the city in 1916.

Ironically, one of Cincinnati's best-known public spaces is not officially part of the city's park system. Located on the north side of Fifth Street, between Vine and Walnut Streets, the site of Fountain Square once was the location of a market. In the mid-19th century, this area became the acknowledged heart of Cincinnati, particularly after the 1871 installation of the fountain that still adorns the square. Businessman Henry Probasco donated the fountain in memory of his brother-in-law and business partner, Tyler Davidson; the female sculpture is titled *The Genius of Water*. This early-20th-century photograph looks east from the fountain and across the paved square. At this time, Fifth Street traffic ran along both sides of the square, but in the area's current configuration, the street jogs around the south side. The view includes numerous buildings no longer standing, but the square, much changed, remains the principal gathering place in downtown Cincinnati.

Public parks had their start in Cincinnati early in the 19th century, thanks to a land donation by brothers John and Benjamin Piatt. A planned market house never was built on the site, so it remained simply a long, narrow green extending between Vine and Elm Streets. The site was flanked on the north and south by the two halves of a street that would become Garfield Place in 1882 in memory of Ohio-born president James A. Garfield, who was assassinated the previous year. The land was formally designated a park in 1868, and for a time it was called Garfield Park. In 1915, a statue of Garfield was installed in the park, the work of local sculptor James Niehaus. Another statue, dedicated in 1896, commemorated Pres. William Henry Harrison, who died of pneumonia in 1841, shortly after taking office.

A photograph taken around the late 1930s looks west from the east end of Piatt Park; the lanes of Garfield Place run along both sides of the park. This end of the park is dominated by the statue of Pres. William Henry Harrison, depicting him in military uniform astride a horse. The planting beds are well kept, and the long rows of facing benches are well occupied on this sunny day. The trees are not fully leafed out, suggesting that it is early spring in Cincinnati. The short shadows indicate a time around noon, when one might expect to see Cincinnatians enjoying some time in the park. In the far distance, the spires of St. Peter in Chains Cathedral, Covenant First Presbyterian Church, the Isaac M. Wise Temple, and Cincinnati City Hall all are visible beyond the park's west end.

By 1962, the urban setting around Piatt Park had not changed significantly, but the park itself had. The statue of President Harrison, the work of sculptor Louis Rebisso, still dominates a view to the west, but the park's landscaping has been much simplified, along with the pattern of walkways. The central walk remains, as do the rows of facing benches. Most are empty, so it must not yet be lunchtime. Automobile design also had evolved quite a bit by this time.

The focal point of today's Mount Storm Park is the Temple of Love. It dates to the mid-19th century, when Mount Storm was the private estate of Robert Bowler. Landscape architect Adolph Strauch designed the temple as part of the overall plan for the estate. The temple had a practical purpose, too, serving as a cover on the cistern that collected water for Bowler's gardens and greenhouses.

Adolph Strauch, looking every inch the Old World gentleman, was at one time an Austrian imperial gardener. Strauch lived from 1822 to 1883 and also was known for his design of Graceland Cemetery in Chicago, the resting place of many of that city's most important people. His chance meeting of Robert Bowler in Europe, followed by his chance missing of a train in Cincinnati (see chapter two), resulted in Strauch's undertaking designs for Spring Grove Cemetery and the city's public parks. While Mount Storm would not become a public park until the World War I era, Strauch's early work there provided him the opportunity to transform the estate into a park-like landscape that would set the tone for later development of Cincinnati's parks.

Robert Bowler died in 1902, the result of a carriage accident on the Sycamore Street hill. Bowler's heirs sold the nearly 60-acre Mount Storm estate to the city in 1911, and in 1917 it officially became a public park. Unfortunately Bowler's 1846 home was demolished at that time, but the Temple of Love and Adolph Strauch's landscape designs remain intact. The park is known for its views of the skyline of the city's Clifton area, as well as of the industrialized valley of Mill Creek. It also has what has been called one of the city's best snow sledding hills.

Adolph Strauch played a major role in shaping Burnet Woods, which was located about a mile southeast of Mount Storm in the Clifton area. Judge Jacob Burnet, an early Cincinnati settler, had prospered as a real estate investor and purchased just over 160 acres of rolling wooded land. Located in the hills just over 2 miles directly north of the city's downtown area, this large parcel served as a retreat for Burnet. After his death, his heirs chose to lease (and later sell) the land to the city rather than subdividing and developing it. City park superintendent Strauch, along with engineer Joseph Earnshaw, created minimal improvements that maximized the site's natural features. The new park included a spring-fed lake, winding roads, dense woodlands, and open, grassy areas. When it opened in 1874, Burnet Woods spurred concern among wealthy Clifton residents who feared an influx of urban masses. The city completed purchase of the land in 1881, and Burnet's heirs committed $50,000 to endow the offering of free public concerts. Clearly it was the masses for whom the park was intended.

The first land for Eden Park was acquired in 1859. Described as first in popularity (and fourth in age) among all the city's parks, it also is among the most beautifully landscaped and probably has the most varied buildings and structures. It is remembered as having no "Keep Out" signs, permitting visitors to walk anywhere on the grass. However the park also served the practical purpose pictured in this aerial photograph looking northwest, likely taken in the 1930s or 1940s. Between 1866 and 1878, the city constructed the 12-acre, 96-million-gallon reservoir that dominates this view. One source noted that the overflow level of the reservoir was 238 feet above the low water level of the Ohio River, giving a sufficient head of water to provide adequate pressure for much of the city. The stone wall of eight arches holding back the water was 1,250 feet in length, and it was apparently sturdy enough not to worry the residents of the homes perched below on the side of Mount Adams.

Two

Late-19th-Century Park Development

The second half of the 19th century saw a new approach to the design of Cincinnati parks, primarily through Adolph Strauch, a Prussian-born landscape gardener. In 1851, he gave a tour of his work at the Crystal Palace in London to visitors that included Cincinnatian Robert Bonner Bowler, who had a country estate, Mount Storm, in the Clifton area. Some time later, while Strauch was traveling he missed a train in Cincinnati. He called on Bowler and ended up staying in the Queen City, where he executed a new design for Mount Storm and others for the estates of several of Bowler's friends.

Northwest from Mount Storm across the Mill Creek valley was Spring Grove Cemetery, established in 1845. Modeled after earlier cemeteries in the east, Spring Grove was an example of the new "lawn plan" cemetery design, which took advantage of elevated view sites in scenic locations well outside urban centers. Such cemeteries served more than the dead—they were intended as places of recreation and repose, where visitors could enjoy a rural setting that was also carefully designed to accentuate the beauty of the site and its horticultural adornments, not to mention its monuments and gravestones.

Strauch felt that Spring Grove had not been developed to its full potential; he described it as looking like "a marble yard where monuments are for sale," and he was promptly hired as landscape gardener by the cemetery's managers. In remaking Spring Grove according to lawn plan principles, Strauch not only created a cemetery widely admired today, but also a design philosophy that would inform much of the subsequent development of the Queen City's park system.

Strauch soon became superintendent of the city's parks. Following the city's acquisition of Eden Park and Burnet Woods in the 1860s and 1870s, Strauch developed designs for both, and these large parks expanded Cincinnati's total parklands to 395 acres. This greatly increased park access to more than 216,000 city residents, although considerable controversy arose over spending public funds for park purchases and development. So intense was the debate that no additional parks were created between 1872 and 1903, during which Cincinnati's population continued its rise to 325,902. Despite the innovative designs and persuasive words of people like Adolph Strauch—not to mention his beautiful parks—at the dawn of the 20th century, Cincinnati could offer its citizens only six public parks.

All aboard for Burnet Woods! The event or celebration that triggered the excursion shown here has gone unrecorded, but a literal boatload of Cincinnatians was ready to leave, seen off by a porch load of well wishers in the background. The older uniformed gentlemen could be members of the Grand Army of the Republic, the late-19th-century organization of Civil War veterans. The wagon-borne boat is named for U.S. admiral George Dewey, the "Hero of Manila" during the Spanish-American War, suggesting a date just before the turn of the 20th century. On the other hand, the flag above the boat appears to have 48 stars; if this is so, the date of the photograph would be 1912 or later. In any case, the youngsters especially are sure to enjoy their trip on the calm waters of the pond at Burnet Woods.

Some excursions were closer to home. In the late 19th and early 20th centuries, both the city and private organizations (such as the Cincinnati Woman's Club, whose pool and pavilion can be seen in the above photograph) took efforts to create playgrounds for the city's children. These were often built right in the heart of urban neighborhoods, where access by foot, even for small children, would be relatively easy. The playgrounds often were short on amenities such as trees and grass, but on a hot Cincinnati summer day, a wading pool was much more welcome anyway.

As appealing as parks are in the summer, they can be forbidding in winter. On a typically gray, overcast Ohio day, a layer of snow, leafless trees and plantings, and a frozen pond do not show Lincoln Park at its best. Several decades after this late-19th-century view, this park would be completely remade as part of the Cincinnati Union Terminal project.

On a similarly grim day there is no snow in Eden Park, but the trees are bare, possibly dating this photograph to early spring. The reservoir is filling in this view, which also shows the 1894 pumping station, which drew water from the Ohio River and raised it to the level of the park to keep the reservoir filled. The station also pumped water into the nearby water tower, which also dated from 1894 and is a major Eden Park landmark. The pumping station was shut down in 1907 due to the high level of pollution in the river at the point of the station's water intakes.

From the time it opened, Burnet Woods offered activity on the water. Rental rowboats were a popular attraction. Two well-dressed young men—a father and son, perhaps—soon will have the pond to themselves. Distant buildings hint at the busy city just outside the park's boundaries, but within the park all is rustic and sylvan.

In the colder months, the boats were safely stored, but Burnet Woods was not without its delights. Other parks might be abandoned for the winter, but the pond and shelter house were all it took to attract a crowd of skaters, as evidenced by this 1909 photograph. One does wonder how all those spindly legged boys stayed warm in their short pants and leggings.

In 1943, the Works Progress Administration published a guide to Cincinnati. Its description of Washington Park, which was nearly nine decades old at the time, said, "On warm, sunny days the park benches are filled with people who loaf and invite their souls." That loafing and inviting must have gone on for some time, since it is certainly in evidence in this 1912 scene. Parasols and wide-brimmed hats were *de rigeur* during Cincinnati summers.

The 1894 Eden Park Water Tower dominates a scene that today is considerably more wooded and lush. The 172-foot tower is 370 feet above the level of the Ohio River in Cincinnati. It held water pumped up from the Eden Park Reservoir and fed hydrants and water mains in areas north. Construction of other tanks led to abandonment of the water tower in 1916, but it remains an enduring symbol of Eden Park.

This view south along Eden Park Drive shows the drive being resurfaced in 1915 and includes two of the park's late-19th-century landmarks. The water tower stands atop its hilltop site. Below it is the Melan Arch Bridge, also known as the "Concrete Bridge," which carries a roadway that runs up to the water tower. Until 1907, visitors could climb the tower and have a spectacular view of Cincinnati from its battlements.

A hillside path in Eden Park leads hikers toward the water tower. The date of the photograph is uncertain, but it was taken at some point early in the 20th century, after enough time had passed for the park's trees to grow quite a bit. Well-maintained lawns and abundant shade could be counted on in all the major Cincinnati parks. This view looks north from near Eden Park Drive.

The Cincinnati Art Museum has crowned one of the highest points of Eden Park since 1886. The museum, intended to boost the city's image as a cultured place, was realized in this Romanesque Revival–style building designed by local architect James W. McLaughlin in the 1870s. Note how small the surrounding trees were then. The photograph also provides a dramatic foreground view of a very rough and unfinished Eden Park.

The Elsinore Gate, also known as the Elsinore Tower, dates from 1883 and stands near the Gilbert Avenue entrance to Eden Park. Its designer, Charles Hannaford, was said to have been inspired by Hamlet's castle of the same name. The Elsinore Gate served as a dramatic entrance feature for the park. Its actual purpose was to house valves that controlled the flow of water from the reservoir into the city's water mains.

A summertime view looks south in the natural hollow in Eden Park below the Cincinnati Art Museum, with the foreground dominated by the 1915 bandstand. This structure differs from those in other parks with its enlarged terrace that goes beyond the row of roof-supporting columns, allowing a much larger assemblage of musicians. Perhaps this was because Eden Park typically expected much greater crowds than most other parks.

Three

The Early 20th Century

Only Piatt, Washington, Lincoln, Hopkins, and Eden Parks, along with Burnet Woods, served the people of Cincinnati at the beginning of the 20th century. These parks dated back to the 1870s or earlier and had never had the benefit of management under a city department dedicated only to developing and operating public parks. During the last three decades of the 19th century, Cincinnati made several efforts to create a park board, but none of these lasted more than just a brief time, dissolving into disputes over finances and political favoritism.

The new century, however, would see a complete change of municipal attitudes towards parks and public attitudes toward funding them. The first decade of the century saw creation of a permanent park commission; passage of the first of many levies to support the parks; and, perhaps most importantly, the publication of a master plan for the park system that would capture the imagination of the public and city officials alike.

Landscape architect George Kessler (1862–1923), a German-born New Yorker, designed several major parks and landscapes, including projects in Baltimore, Cleveland, and Kansas City. Demand for his services increased greatly after his work planning the layout of the World's Fair in St. Louis in 1904.

Kessler came to Cincinnati to produce the 1907 master plan for the city's parks, a document that would shape the park system from then on. As the 20th century progressed, Cincinnati's citizens would see tremendous growth in the number and quality of their parks. Existing parks received improvements such as pavilions and bandstands, while new parks were created all over the city, often through the donation of private land.

Cincinnati's population would exceed 400,000 by 1920, and by 1930 it would total 451,000, a direct result of the continued growth of the city's industrial base. In 1920, the United States reached a significant milestone: more people lived in urban than in rural areas, according to that year's census. Some 68 cities had populations over 100,000; modern urban American life had arrived. That was certainly the case in the Queen City, where the need and the demand for park space was answered most generously.

They hardly seem dressed for the adventure on which they are embarking, but that does not seem to bother these Cincinnati children spending a day in the wilds of Ault Park. The photograph caption reads, "Rustic bridge over Redbank Creek with children beneath." The creek appears to have little or no water during the dry summer season, and the bridge is indeed rustic.

August 1913 found this group of friends enjoying a picnic at Ault Park on the far east side of Cincinnati. The back of the photograph reads, "Girls Picnic Party Under Big Maple Tree." All attendees are dressed in light-colored summer dresses, and they have assembled a formidable array of picnic baskets. Also on the back of the photograph, in another hand, is the plea, "Will someone offer identifications?" Unfortunately, no one has.

The Eckerlin Express Company provided a truck to carry "the poor from a downtown district" to Burnet Woods for the 1915 municipal picnic. Titled "A Truck-Load of Happiness," this photograph shows a less-than-happy driver and mostly subdued-looking children; presumably everyone's mood improved as they approached Clifton and Burnet Woods. Taking children to city parks was a common philanthropic activity intended to give them a wholesome setting for recreation and fun.

Later that same day, everyone does indeed seem to be having fun, at least at the competition described on this photograph as "a hot race for boys" in Burnet Woods. This was the final race, apparently won by the hatted and smiling lad, third from the left, about to break the tape. Alas, his name has been lost to posterity. A few spectators find the camera more interesting than the race.

A slightly grainy photograph shows a view of an old Burnet Woods shelter house. Its design is a little different from many others, featuring stone pillars supporting paired wooden columns. The broad roof overhang provided plenty of shade, but the many steps allowed those who wished to get some sun.

One of Cincinnati's finest appears to have corralled a couple of desperadoes in this 1912 photograph taken in Burnet Woods. Whether the three are simply conversing is not known, but it must be noted that the boy on the left has a bit of a "who, me?" look on his face, while the other looks distinctly guilty of something. Note also the brakeless bicycles and the shared metal drinking cups attached to chains on the ornate drinking fountain, two things not permitted by today's health and safety laws. At left beyond the policeman is some seating for the park's bandstand.

An old view of one of the stone and wood structures in Burnet Woods shows how well its design fit in with the natural setting of the park. This was true throughout the city park system, where the careful blending of nature and man-made amenities was always the goal. Even the light and utility poles seem to be made as thin and unobtrusive as possible, so that the park's natural assets dominated the scene.

In an undated early-20th-century photograph, Jefferson Avenue, along the north side of Burnet Woods, is being paved. Paving bricks or stone blocks were the standard in the days before asphalt and concrete became more common, and they survive today under countless urban streets in Cincinnati and elsewhere. This view looks west along Jefferson, and the area being paved appears to be an entrance drive into the park.

Visitors to Burnet Woods around 1915 found this nicely paved roadway into the park. As automobiles became more reliable and affordable after about 1910, demand for them surged, as did the demand for hard-paved streets and roads. Unlike Jefferson Avenue in the preceding photograph, the road surface here appears to be concrete and asphalt.

Burnet Woods hosted a large contingent during the 1915 municipal picnic. This photograph of a group of attentive people is titled "A Section of the Crowd, Listening to an Address in Burnet Woods." There is no record of the speaker or the topic. Some in the crowd are listening, but others gaze at the camera, and in the left background, men in summertime straw boaters carry on a conversation. There is no indication of what the prize would be for finding a green tag on a drinking cup.

A winter visit to Burnet Woods shows the 1911 bandstand (also called a music pavilion) in quiet repose. It would not be too many more months before the leaves would come out, the grass would turn green, and the crowds and musicians would return for yet another summer concert series. Cincinnati's parks often benefited from bequests from donors who wanted to support free public concerts, and the park board responded by building appropriate facilities.

An early-20th-century view of the Miami and Erie Canal in downtown Cincinnati depicts a quiet scene that was all too common in the canal's later years. Having lost its high-value freight traffic to railroads and interurbans, the canal in the early 20th century still had some usefulness as a means of carrying bulk materials such as sand and rock. Indeed, the State of Ohio made a substantial investment in rebuilding much of the statewide canal system just before 1910. This was not because it had a future as a transportation network, but the system did generate revenues from waterpower leases to canal-side factories and mills. All this would end in 1913, when that year's devastating spring floods destroyed many miles of canals.

This photograph (taken between Main and Walnut Streets) and the preceding one depict a short-lived effort to keep the Miami and Erie Canal operating. In 1901, the Miami and Erie Deep Waterway Association was incorporated to introduce "electric mules" to replace horses and mules as canal power. The idea was that electric power would make boat movement efficient enough that the canal could still be a useful means of transport. In both photographs, a close look reveals a railroad track along the right bank, on the towpath of the canal. It was along this track that the electric locomotives—14 feet long, equivalent to the power of 80 mules, built very low to fit under bridges—would travel, hauling boats. Unfortunately, the "mules" pulled the boats so fast that waves eroded the canal bank under the track, and overspending on the system also doomed the enterprise. In fact, these photographs were made after the operation shut down and the overhead wire was removed. It was all gone by 1905.

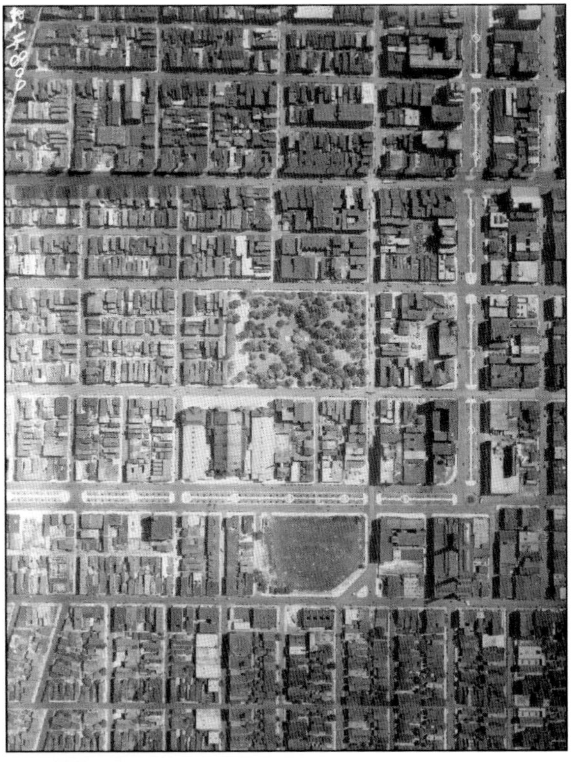

An aerial photograph from about 1928 shows how the Miami and Erie Canal was replaced by Central Parkway. North is to the left; the parkway comes into the downtown area from the north and then turns east. The Over-the-Rhine neighborhood is in the upper left of the photograph, east and north of the parkway.

This 1928 photograph looks east from the corner where Central Parkway turns to run east along the north side of downtown Cincinnati. A hazy Mount Adams is faintly visible in the far distance. The parkway provided improved mobility for cars and quicker access to the city's north side, as well as eliminating the problem of the outmoded and noxious canal.

The Twin Lakes are in the northeast corner of Eden Park, perched near the top of the high bluff above Columbia Parkway and the Ohio River. This photograph looks east along the Ohio side of the river, with the Kentucky floodplain at the right edge of the view. The distant shadowy shapes on the river are steamboats; one might even be the famous *Island Queen* on one her runs to and from the Coney Island amusement park, located several miles upriver from downtown Cincinnati. The Twin Lakes once were the site of a stone quarry and are linked by a concrete bridge dating from 1903. The bridge is just visible at left center in the upper photograph and is shown in a closer view in the lower photograph.

Eden Park Drive runs southeast off Gilbert Avenue next to the former Baldwin Piano Company building. In 1915, this was the view looking uphill along the drive from just off Gilbert, while well-dressed Cincinnatians made their way into the park for the 1915 municipal picnic. Of interest in the distance is the west side of the Stone Arch Bridge, built in 1874 to carry a roadway across Eden Park Drive. In the early 20th century, the bridge had another bridge built upon it to serve the Zoo-Eden streetcar line. This line was famous because its cars rode an incline up Mount Adams in order to reach the hilltop portion of its route. The support towers for the trolley wire rise above the deck of the streetcar bridge in this view looking southeast.

The view looking back to the northwest shows the east side of the Stone Arch Bridge and its streetcar bridge, with a building along Gilbert Avenue visible in the distance. The Cincinnati Art Museum is up the hill to the left, out of view. This and the preceding view show how the bridge forced vehicle traffic on the wide Eden Park Drive to funnel down to pass through the arch. This no doubt helped lead to its demise only two decades after this 1929 photograph. The bridge is visible at the upper left in the aerial photograph on page 22, which was taken some years before its demolition.

Another view from the 1915 municipal picnic provides a close-up look at the Elsinore Tower (also called the Elsinore Gate) at Eden Park. The scene is described on the back of the photograph as "Crowds entering park through Elsinore Gate. A steady stream of people, all day long, up Elsinore Walk to Eden Park." The 1883 date stone is clearly visible above the arch through which people passed on the long climb up from Gilbert Avenue. Regardless of whether this is an accurate rendering of Hamlet's Danish castle, it has become a well-loved Cincinnati landmark.

This photograph, which looks east into the haze of the Ohio River Valley, shows the Emma Louise Schmidlapp wing of the Cincinnati Art Museum. It was completed in 1907, a gift from Cincinnati businessman Jacob G. Schmidlapp in memory of his daughter. The wing was designed by Daniel H. Burnham's Chicago architectural firm, well known for his Beaux-Arts creations for the 1893 World's Columbian Exposition in Chicago.

Eden Park's natural amphitheater around its new music pavilion has filled with visitors in summer dress for the 1915 municipal picnic. The nearby Eden Park Reservoir had been drained for repairs, providing a setting for thousands of dancers. The municipal picnic drew about a third of the city's population to Eden, Ault, and Mount Echo Parks and Burnet Woods. The music pavilion lasted until 1960, when it was replaced by the Seasongood Pavilion.

Looking south along Eden Park Drive, this photograph shows the Melan Arch Bridge and one of its guardian eagles, which were removed from the old chamber of commerce building that was destroyed by fire in 1911. The granite birds first went to the zoological society and then to Eden Park, where they were put in place to crown the four end pillars of the retaining walls along the park's drive at the bridge.

A photograph dating from not long after 1912 looks southwest from the Melan Arch Bridge and shows the tidy lawns and orderly plantings of Eden Park. One of the bridge's retaining walls and chamber of commerce eagles can be seen at lower center. In the distance, the homes, businesses, and institutions of Mount Adams bask in the summer sun.

This view from around the early 1900s looks southwest toward the barely visible west basin of the Eden Park Reservoir. At left center is the 1904 Spring House Gazebo, built over a spring that was supposed to have medicinal qualities. Today the Playhouse in the Park, which presides over the Mount Adams neighborhood, crowns the high ridge in the background.

A closer view of Eden Park's Spring House Gazebo reveals its ornate design and varied materials. The scalloped arches are reminiscent of the architecture of India, while the little onion dome evokes images of Russia. Built in a period when many building designs could only be called eclectic, the gazebo certainly drew its inspiration from far and wide.

Alms Park, originally Frederick H. Alms Memorial Park, grew from a 1916 donation of land made by the widow of the builder of the Alms Hotel and partner in the Alms and Doepke department store. This view looks up the park drive to a high point of land, where a pavilion was completed in 1929. The terrace and walks were designed by landscape architect Albert D. Taylor of Cleveland.

A closer view of the Alms Park Pavilion shows the Italian Renaissance influence of its design, which shared characteristics with the designs for the pavilions at Ault and Mount Echo Parks.

Rustic bridges and paths abounded in Alms Park. The high bluff on which the park sits was once known as Bald Hill, the legend being that native tribes had cleared the trees in order to watch for approaching white settlers. Even allowing for the fact that it is winter, these views show that by the 1920s or 1930s, the tree cover in the park still was fairly sparse. What a contrast this was with the busy, dense, noisy, and hurried city just downriver.

Ault Park was named for and donated by Levi Ault and his wife, Ida May. Ault was in the printing ink business and was on the board of park commissioners at the time George Kessler developed the 1907 park plan. During Ault's service as president of the board between 1908 and 1926, the city's parks went from a total of just under 370 to over 2,200 acres. Ault made his first land donation for a park in 1911. The park would eventually total 224 acres. Landscape architect A. D. Taylor developed this impressive plan, dominated by a large pavilion at the east end (north is to the right on the plan), for the southern half of the park.

Development of Ault Park required the removal of several existing homes. This was unfortunate because some were fairly impressive. But most people would agree that the loss was acceptable because the park became such an asset to the city.

A view looking east in Ault Park shows the pavilion under construction. It was the largest of the three Cincinnati park pavilions inspired by Italian Renaissance architecture (the others were in Alms and Mount Echo Parks). All three, which have been carefully restored, still serve park visitors today. The wide stairs flanking a cascading fountain made the Ault Park Pavilion unique.

Landscape architect Albert D. Taylor (1884–1951) had his office in Cleveland and worked on Cincinnati park projects from 1927 to 1941. He designed the landscapes for Alms, Ault, and Mount Echo Parks, as well as Fleischmann Gardens. Other Cincinnati projects included the landscaped approach to Union Terminal and work for the Cincinnati Art Museum and the Garden Club of Cincinnati. One of his most important projects was the site of the Pentagon in Washington in 1943.

A large proportion of park visitors used the city's vast streetcar system. This view of Ault Park is a bit gloomy and must have been taken on an overcast summer day, but it gives a sense of how much people relied on the streetcars. No fewer than seven cars are disgorging their loads onto the wooden platform. By 1951, streetcars were gone from the city.

Any children on the passing streetcar probably wished they were in the Inwood Park wading pool and not climbing the Vine Street hill. It was high summer early in the 20th century. Despite fears of mysterious diseases such as polio, to which children seemed especially susceptible when they got wet and chilled, Cincinnati's urban playgrounds and pools drew throngs during the hot months.

Taken around the same time as the preceding photograph, another view of the wading pool at Inwood Park shows the contrast between today's swimwear and what was considered appropriate around 1911. At least as much water has been splashed out of the pool as has stayed in it. Inwood Park still serves the city today and is on the east side of Vine Street not far below McMillan Street and the University of Cincinnati.

A former stone quarry became the site of Inwood Park, located on Vine Street as it climbed the hill out of the central city. The initial land purchase was in 1904, with more land added over the next 10 years. George Kessler planned the park, providing for playground equipment, plantings, and a pool that proved very popular with neighborhood children. The park had a shelter house, also described as a pavilion. It is shown here in its original form, a single-story building with an open pergola on the roof. It took its current form in 1913, when it received a full second story and a tile roof. It was in one of the doorways of this structure that the photograph on page 72 was made.

Fleischmann Gardens is in Avondale at the northwest corner of Forest and Washington Avenues. Just over 4 acres in size, the park was the site of an impressive mansion owned by Charles Fleischmann, founder of the Fleischmann Yeast Company. His heirs donated the land to the city in 1925, along with a maintenance fund. The mansion was demolished, and today an ornate entrance gate on Washington Avenue marks the main access point. The park contains what is said to be the largest gingko tree in Ohio.

Inside Fleischmann Gardens was the broad walkway known as the *allee*, a French term for a pathway flanked by trees or plantings. Stone paving and pillars add a sense of high quality in the design and execution of this small piece of the public realm.

For many years, Fleischmann Gardens was known for its lily ponds, shown here on a sunny summer day. In this view, errant visitors' feet appear to have pushed the low wire fence out of line, but it has done its job of protecting the plantings.

Ducks, swans, and humans all are enjoying Lincoln Park on a sunny day early in the 20th century. Today highway construction, urban renewal, and new building construction have completely changed the face of this part of Cincinnati.

An early-20th-century view reveals that Lytle Park, located at the eastern end of the city's downtown, once had a columned bandstand (visible behind the strolling people). This park was dedicated on July 6, 1907, in honor of Brig. Gen. William Lytle, whose family home stood on the site. The City of Cincinnati acquired the land for the park in 1905. It was intended to benefit the children of poor inner-city residents.

High on Price Hill, Mount Echo Park provides spectacular views of the city and the valley of the Ohio River (see page 12). The park, established in 1908, contains more than 80 acres and is reached by means of Elberon Avenue. By 1913, this spectacular stone retaining wall, with its entrance steps and driveway, was well into construction. The old foundation, wooden steps, and precariously perched outbuildings give a sense of what hillside living was like.

A 1913 photograph looking uphill shows workmen busy on the Mount Echo retaining wall. Mount Echo was said to have been named for the resonance of the cliffs that rose some 300 feet above the Ohio River. By the early 1900s, the area around Mount Echo had developed considerably. Following the Kessler Plan, the city acquired the first 40-plus acres and later added more land. The Elberon Avenue streetcar line made access easy for area residents.

By 1915, Mount Echo Park's retaining wall was complete. It is one of the most distinctive in the park system. It has the quite practical purpose of holding back the steep hillside that otherwise would have tended to slip and collapse, especially in extremely wet weather. Incorporating the entrance steps and driveway into the wall, and the gracefully lettered identification sign with raised metal letters, only contributed to the quality and character of the park. The wall and entrance remain in use today.

The pavilion in Mount Echo Park is one of only a few Cincinnati park buildings constructed in the Italian Renaissance style. It was completed in 1928 in a design by local architects Rendigs, Panzer, and Martin, designers of the YWCA structure at 898 Walnut Street. The pavilion housed a concession stand and restrooms. The terrace and landscaping around the pavilion were designed by Cleveland landscape architect A. D. Taylor.

A view through the loggia of the Mount Echo Park Pavilion reveals its Italian inspiration. The arch was a building innovation from the days of the Romans. The classical columns supporting the pavilion's roof were drawn directly from Roman practice, as were the engaged columns (known as pilasters) on the pavilion's exterior walls. The views from the pavilion make the drive (or walk) up to Mount Echo Park a worthwhile undertaking.

Vote "Yes" for a Park Commission

SEPARATE BALLOT—PLACE X OPPOSITE "YES"

Your "yes" **will place Parks and Playgrounds** **in charge of a continuous non-political commission.**
Your "yes" **will not mean an increase** **on the tax levy.**
Your "yes" **will not mean** **the issue of Park Bonds unless desired and voted for by the people.**
Your "yes" **will not create new salaried officers.**

What Is a Park Commission?

A Park Commission is a body consisting of three men, to be appointed by the Mayor. They will serve without salary. They are not to be subject to any local political changes. They are to be selected from among our most public spirited citizens of the highest reputation and standing.

This Park Commission is to develop and follow a definite *Park Plan,* and it is to have full charge of all our present *Parks* and *Playgrounds,* as well as the selection of new ones. *It means that the children will be recognized;* that they *will have safe places, besides the streets to play.* Safe places to wade and swim, besides the canal and river. The establishment of a *Park Commission* is in line with what has been adopted by all the leading cities of the country.

The appointment of a *Park Commission* has been unanimously endorsed by the press of our city, irrespective of politics or language. We append quotations from each of the papers, English and German:

CINCINNATI ENQUIRER—All voters can and should unite on one proposition—that of voting "Yes" for a Park Commission.

COMMERCIAL TRIBUNE—The vote on the Park Commission should be in the affirmative and largely so. If the vote is in the negative, Cincinnati would be placed far down on the roll of progressive cities.

TIMES STAR—An unfavorable vote on the proposed Park Commission would be a real disaster to Cincinnati.

CINCINNATI POST—Voters will perform only half their duty if they fail to vote for the proposed Park Commission. It is the duty of every resident to secure an overwhelming vote for this commission.

CINCINNATI VOLKSBLATT—We strongly recommend all citizens to vote "Yes" on the proposition for a Park Commission.

CINCINNATI FREIE PRESSE—The Park Commission should be favored by all citizens. Not a single reason can be advanced against it, and many strong arguments can be made in favor of the plan.

All the Commercial, Industrial and Improvement Associations of the city, and also the Associated Organizations, have endorsed it.

THE GREATER PARK LEAGUE,

T. J. MOFFETT,	L. A. AULT,	NAT. HENCHMAN DAVIS,
GEORGE PUCHTA,	A. J. CONROY,	IRWIN M. KROHN,
R. E. MORRISON,	GEORGE F. DIETERLE,	JULIUS FLEISCHMANN,

Executive Committee.

74

Establishment of a park commission (today called the park board) in the early 1900s was a critical step in putting Cincinnati's parks on a sound political and financial footing. This flyer put out by the Greater Park League encouraged a favorable vote on the issue. The city's citizens did just that, 57,941 of them voting yes, against the 11,744 who voted no.

Owl's Nest Park, located on a modest 10-acre parcel on Madison Road in the East Walnut Hills/Evanston area, was the site of the Perkins family homestead. James H. Perkins had settled here in 1845 and had a varied career that included work as an attorney, a newspaper editor, and a congregational minister. He disappeared from a moored barge on the Ohio River in 1849 in a presumed suicide. In 1905, sons Charles and Edward Perkins donated land for a park at the site. The wrought iron fence and gates were sold for scrap during World War II.

Construction of Victory Parkway was, to say the least, disruptive, as is any large public improvement. A description on the back of this photograph describes the view as "Gilbert Avenue intersection before paving was started" and has the date of March 29, 1915. The view looks north, roughly, and shows the "shoo-fly" the local streetcar line had to use while the parkway was being built. The location is north of Walnut Hills, and this photograph shows some of the large suburban districts that began to grow in the early 20th century, as streetcar lines and automobiles made it feasible for people to live out in pleasant, hilly areas while still working and shopping in the central city. Projects such as Victory Parkway would serve to reinforce that trend.

This view of Victory Parkway under construction is marked only with the description "from RR bridge," which would place it between Gilbert and Rockdale Avenues, just north of today's Interstate Route 71. The wide pavement, gentle grades, and graceful curves were a huge contrast with the narrow, hilly, and confusing streets early automobile drivers were used to navigating in Cincinnati.

The short-lived Avondale Athletic Club, which stood on Dana Avenue, is shown here. In 1903, the club closed, and the predecessor of Xavier University acquired the land. Several of Xavier's buildings now fill this view, and Victory Parkway passes through the area off to the right. The parkway originally was called Bloody Run Parkway, and was renamed Victory Parkway in 1921. The creek called Bloody Run took its name from a 1794 attack by Native Americans on a group of men leading packhorses through the creek valley.

In December 1927, this view north on Victory Parkway, not far from its north end, must have been taken on a quiet Sunday morning. The wide, grassy tree lawns, with sidewalks set well back from the traffic lanes, enhanced the suburban housing that was already filling up the area along the new roadway.

In 1912, Woodward Park was getting a fresh gravel road surface. Animal power for vehicles survived a surprisingly long time into the 20th century. Indeed, the heavy steel gravel wagon these mules were pulling is of some interest. A close look reveals large manually operated brake shoes near the tops of the rear wheels.

Among the many early-20th-century park improvements were several music pavilions, or bandstands. In 1910, Washington Park received just such a structure, which shared some common characteristics with others in the park system. These included an octagonal form, supporting columns, and a low-pitched clay tile roof. Varying architectural details, however, made each music pavilion unique. In this winter view looking northwest, the Cincinnati Music Hall looms in the right background.

Four

THE DEPRESSION ERA

The Great Depression of the 1930s was one of the most disruptive economic downturns in U.S. history. It was a period of joblessness, failed businesses, lost fortunes, and foreclosed homes and farms. At the same time, innovative—if controversial—ideas at the national level, which were intended to get both people and the economy working again, presented a unique opportunity for cities such as Cincinnati. To be sure, the Queen City suffered at least as much as the rest of the nation from the ravages of the Depression, but when President Roosevelt's relief programs were made law and significant federal funding became available, Cincinnati was quick to capitalize. From the alphabet soup of new agencies and programs—PWA, CCC, WPA—the city successfully sought funds and undertook projects that significantly improved and enhanced its park system.

Of 135 buildings and structures in Cincinnati's parks, nearly half were erected between 1929 and 1943. Projects completed in the early years (before the early 1930s) typically were not federally supported. Instead they were a continuation of the local funding and aggressive development efforts that grew out of the 1907 park plan and the 1925 plan for the city of Cincinnati, which placed great importance on the continued development of the park system. Once the federal programs were underway, however, Cincinnati was able to garner a generous amount of funding, and this resulted in creation of some of the park system's most enduring and attractive features.

Two designers, one an architect and one a landscape architect, played a key role during this period in shaping the city's parks. R. Carl Freund, a Cincinnati architect, worked for the park board for nearly 30 years, until his death in 1959, and was responsible for 37 building designs. Albert D. Taylor of Cleveland began doing landscape plans for the park board in the late 1920s and continued until 1941.

All of this meant that the 1930s, and even the early years of World War II, were very good for Cincinnati's parks. The buildings, structures, and other improvements created during this time put the park system in excellent shape for the heavy use it would receive in the prosperous postwar years.

It is not known whether these children are among "the poor" who well-meaning citizens and groups took to city parks and playgrounds for summer recreation, but they undoubtedly are typical urban kids of the era before World War II. The photograph caption describes the scene as "Two little girls eating ice cream cones at boys entrance of shelter house." The setting is Inwood Park on the Vine Street hill. Boys this age must have been wondering if they would ever be allowed to leave their short pants and long stockings behind for more manly clothing. Earlier views of Inwood Park are on pages 57 and 58.

Both the excellence of its parks and the skills of Cincinnati's citizens as gardeners may have influenced the choice of the city as host of the National Flower Show in 1931. The event was held at the music hall, where some of the exhibits featured stonework that looked surprisingly like what had been built in recent years in many city parks.

During tough economic times, a nature walk could brighten the spirit. This well-dressed party hardly looks as though it should be tramping up a streambed, but careful stepping on flat rocks would generally keep the feet dry. The gentleman at right has protected his legs with puttees, an article not found in most clothing stores today.

At 1501 Eden Park Drive is the Krohn Conservatory, built in 1933 and named in honor of Irwin M. Krohn, who served on the board of park commissioners from 1912 until 1948. In this construction photograph, the pylon at the right is the conservatory's heating plant chimney, with geometric art deco styling. In the distance, the Eden Park Water Tower rises above the trees and shows a stark contrast in architectural design.

The completed Krohn Conservatory opened as the Eden Park Greenhouse on April 1, 1933 (one day after the dedication of Cincinnati Union Terminal). In 1937, the conservatory was renamed for Irwin Krohn, who died in 1948 at the age of nearly 80 years. The conservatory has an area of 22,000 square feet and features a palm house with tropical plants, fishponds, and areas with desert plants and orchids.

When Victory Parkway was dedicated in 1929, it was a beautifully designed and broad paved roadway. Before long it would gain this shelter house, dating from 1935 and boasting a large sign reading "Victory Parkway Shelter," which provided drinking water and public restrooms. Located at Rockdale Avenue, it was built of stone in a modified and more refined version of the park rustic designs found in many of Cincinnati's parks. It still stands today.

At three-tenths of an acre, Auburn Triangle, shown here in the 1930s, is not a very large part of the Cincinnati park system. Located between the University of Cincinnati and Mount Auburn, it is nevertheless a welcome oasis in a heavily developed part of the city.

The Federal Art Project was one of many Depression-era programs intended to stimulate employment in various fields. Cincinnati became particularly adept at securing federal funding from various programs for improvements all over the city's park system. This included funding for construction of buildings and other structures, as well as for work crews to build trails and plant trees in places such as Mount Airy Forest.

Cincinnati's federally funded park improvements blended nicely with some of the work of the Federal Art Project, as witnessed by these promotional posters from the period. The design on page 76 invokes a higher authority, against a stylized oak tree backdrop, to encourage conservation. The design on this page depicts Ohio's state tree, the buckeye.

The Michael Mullen Memorial Bandstand in Lytle Park, located at the east edge of the downtown area, was an outstanding example of art deco design. Looking like an offspring of Cincinnati Union Terminal, the bandstand was completed in 1935 and was located along what, at the time, was the south edge of the park. It was named in honor of a long-serving Eighth Ward city councilman. The bandstand's backside can be seen at lower center in the aerial photograph on page 98. These two views show the bandstand's front. It is no longer standing.

Parkers Woods is a 62-acre park located between Spring Grove Cemetery and Hamilton Avenue (U.S. Route 127). This 1934 photograph of an open shelter under construction there shows how the many park rustic–style structures in the Cincinnati park system were built.

This comfort station in Stanbery Park in Mount Washington has a design typical of enclosed structures from the Depression era. Considered an example of park rustic design, it was completed in 1940 and paid for with federal funds.

Rapid Run Park is in West Price Hill and has this large pavilion set above a reflecting pond. The five segmental-arched openings provide a pleasant setting for park visitors and a welcome respite from the sometimes-fierce storms that can come up quickly during Midwest summers. The building was completed in 1941 and in this photograph has its original shingle roof. That roof has since been covered with a metal one.

The Civilian Conservation Corps (CCC) came into being during the Depression for two main reasons: it created jobs for the vast army of the unemployed in the early 1930s, and it addressed a major national problem of deforestation and soil erosion due to poor land management practices. President Roosevelt acted quickly to work with Congress to pass the Emergency Conservation Work Act in early 1933. The CCC soon came into being, overcoming huge logistical problems involved with moving available labor to areas needing conservation work. By 1942, the CCC was credited with planting some three billion trees among all the other work it accomplished.

In his 1907 park plan for Cincinnati, George Kessler had urged quick acquisition of large parcels of land before growing development pressure pushed prices out of reach. Kessler had not specified the location where Mount Airy Forest would be created, but as early as 1911, the city began acquiring land several miles northwest of the downtown area with the idea of establishing a major park. The land purchases involved some worked-out farms like the one in the photograph above. It took several years, but as funding became available and work went forward, Mount Airy Forest began to take shape. It would become recognized as the first municipal reforestation project in the United States.

In 1935, Cincinnati obtained the services of a CCC crew composed entirely of young African American men. Over several years, they would plant more than a million trees and would erect numerous shelters, pavilions, and other buildings in Mount Airy Forest. Other work included construction of roads and a water system for the park.

The CCC workers lived in an isolated camp within the boundaries of Mount Airy Forest. The workers were housed in dormitories and were served by facilities such as dining and recreation halls. These were intended as temporary structures but remained after the CCC camp closed. When Interstate Route 74 was built through the middle of Mount Airy Forest, the CCC camp buildings were moved and still stand today on a hill above that highway.

One worn-out property acquired to create Mount Airy Forest was called the Schunk farm, shown in the photograph above. Other farms acquired for the park were cleared of all buildings, and so was this one, with the exception of the fieldstone farmhouse, which dated to 1869. That building was rehabilitated and became Pine Ridge Lodge in Mount Airy Forest (below). The rehabilitation's design was very much in keeping with the rustic character of much of what was being built in the park, including the bare tree trunk posts supporting the gabled half-story above the large added porch. CCC crews did the renovation with federal funds.

Five

The Mid- to Late 20th Century

As the Depression ended with the onset of World War II, the nation's attention turned to achieving victory. While this effort was all consuming, Americans still needed the rest, relaxation, and recreational opportunities offered by public parks. During the war, the Queen City's park system would not see the same intensity of development and improvements as in earlier decades. However even in the war years there were new parks and some new buildings and structures.

It was after the war and the onset of a new period of prosperity that the pace began to pick up again. Shelters, pavilions, an arboretum, and more were added to Cincinnati's park system in the 1950s and into the 1960s. Some of this work occurred into the 1970s, notably the innovative construction of a downtown freeway under Lytle Park. But as the final two decades of the 20th century approached, the city's park system had largely matured.

The challenge at that point was caring for what had already been put in place, and this was not always possible. Some buildings and some areas had to be closed to the public. In some cases, the parks seemed on the verge of losing some of their major landmarks.

Fortunately Cincinnati City Council approved a new parks and greenways plan in 1992, and along with it came a new commitment to preserve the legacy of a great park system. Over several years, significant efforts have been put into restoration of structures, renovation and enhancement of parks and facilities, and better overall care for all the many components of the parks. By the turn of the 21st century, Cincinnati's park system was recognized as one of the nation's best.

The Works Progress Administration, one of several federal Depression-era programs whose projects greatly enhanced the look, character, and quality of Cincinnati's parks, left its calling card at various locations. It would not be long after this date stone was set that the Depression period would end and a new economic stimulus—war—would once again remake the nation. When peace returned, the Queen City's great park system would see a new period of prosperity.

Few buildings in Cincinnati's parks provided a greater contrast in design than the Temple of Love in Mount Storm Park (page 18) and its pavilion, shown above. Completed in 1935, this building was the work of Samuel Hannaford and Sons. Built of squared stone blocks, the Mount Storm pavilion had a spare, plain character evocative of the new, modern era of architecture that would evolve out of the war years and the vibrant 1950s that followed.

Some park improvements after World War II were incremental, while others were complete remakes. Hopkins Park was an example of the latter. Above shows the park as it existed for a long time, dutifully complying with its donor's requirement that it be "kept forever free of buildings." The redone park is in the lower photograph, still with abundant trees as the donor also required, but with more useful public spaces and better amenities.

French Memorial Park in Amberley Village was once known as Reachmont Farm, the home of Herbert G. French, a longtime official of the Procter and Gamble Company. After his passing in 1942, the park board took possession of the 276-acre farm. French's house, which consisted of an old farmhouse and many later additions, today is the park's centerpiece. The park is emblematic of the large country estates that once made up Amberley Village.

Providing a stark contrast with the early-20th-century French House, the open shelter at French Park, built in 1954, is a long, V-shaped building with a low-pitched roof and little character. Its debt to the numerous prewar shelters and pavilions in the park system is obvious, but it is entirely a product of the modern era.

Bramble Park, today managed by the Cincinnati Recreation Commission, is in far eastern Cincinnati, just north of Fairfax and Mariemont. Its shelter, depicted here in an architect's rendering and as completed in 1962, was the essence of modern design at the time. Only in its open plan, its broad overhanging roof, and its use of masonry walls and pillars could it be considered a descendant of the park rustic designs that dominated the architecture of the park system in the Depression era. The shelter is no longer standing.

Deep in Mount Airy Forest, the 1948 Oak Ridge Lodge is the second of three lodges built in the park. Featuring a terrace and an assembly room that can open to the outdoors, the lodge is ideal for group gatherings. It is a product of its time, with modern detailing, a low profile, and a nearly flat roof. It recalls the prairie style of architecture as practiced by Frank Lloyd Wright and others.

In April 1949, the Colerain Avenue waiting station in Mount Airy Forest looked more like a puzzle than a building project. R. Carl Freund designed the structure by blending the park rustic and art moderne styles. In this view, workers have completed the pair of massive stone pillars that would support the roof. Once finished, the building provided restrooms and a sheltered waiting area for people traveling to Mount Airy Forest by bus.

The Hauck Botanical Gardens are at 2625 Reading Road in Avondale. In 1924, the property became home to Cornelius Hauck, a director of the Little Miami Railroad and well-known railroad historian. He was also a park commissioner. His interest in botany led to creation of an arboretum on his estate, which was left to the park board with a trust for maintenance after Hauck's death in 1967. This 1968 photograph shows a fanciful frame gazebo in the Hauck Botanical Gardens.

These park workers are planting a tree at the Alms Park Overlook in December 1944. In the spring, the tree will provide some shade for visitors enjoying the unsurpassed view from the overlook, ranging from an upriver view that takes in Lunken Field and the valley of the Little Miami River, to downriver views of Kentucky and Cincinnati's east side. The vantage point here is more than 300 feet above the Ohio River.

The Trailside Museum (today the Trailside Nature Center) was constructed in 1939 with federal funding in a design by architect R. Carl Freund. Located in Burnet Woods, the building today hosts many nature classes for both children and adults. This photograph was made after the 1975 project that replaced the original leaky flat roof with a pitched one.

A view of the west side of the Trailside Nature Center shows the structure with its original flat roof. The rounded corners of the rough stone walls gave it a "streamlined" and modern look while still reflecting the rustic and natural character of the building materials. Its design probably owed much to the innovative work of architect Frank Lloyd Wright.

A unique feature of Burnet Woods is the H. H. Richardson Monument. Architect Henry Hobson Richardson designed the 1888 chamber of commerce building, which was destroyed by fire in 1911. Stones from the rubble were set aside to erect an observatory, which never happened. The stones were rediscovered in the late 1960s, and the University of Cincinnati's architecture school had a competition seeking reuse proposals. This was the winning design.

Elsewhere in Burnet Woods, on another day, busy hands are hard at work on a project involving what appears to be buckeye nuts, which are unfit for human consumption and not useful for much of anything else. This has not deterred these hard-working students at the Trailside Museum, not one of whom is smiling. One traditional use of buckeyes is in making clocks in the shape of Ohio, with the nuts marking the hours.

Some of the elegant detailing of the Stone Arch Bridge in Eden Park is visible in this view of its demolition in the summer of 1949. It boasted classical columns and round-arched arcading. The tooth-like projections below the stone handrail were false machicolations, intended to resemble the slots through which the defenders of a castle could drop weapons on attacking enemies. See pages 46 and 47 for views of the bridge in happier times.

What youngster has not dreamed of a ride on a horse or, better yet, a pony? On this summer day in 1984, the Eden Park ponies have a full load of happy riders. Some of these children would be approaching 40 or so today; one hopes that they still have good memories of Eden Park.

One of the more unusual structures in the Cincinnati park system is the pavilion at Bellevue Hill Park in Clifton Heights. Completed in 1955, it was among the last designs by R. Carl Freund. The pavilion combined a bandstand and an area for dancing, its most distinctive feature being the three flat concrete canopies set in planting beds and supported by clusters of concrete columns.

Under the canopies, geometric openings create an intriguing pattern of light and shadow on the pavement. This photograph, probably taken not long after the structure's completion, shows some well-dressed midday visitors; note all the low walls suitable for sitting and enjoying the view from the hilltop park.

Reflecting the geometric forms, flat roofs, and low-profile designs typical of park structures in the period following World War II, the comfort station in Washington Park, shown here in 1948, contrasts with the nearby Cincinnati Music Hall and other 19th-century buildings around the park.

Miles Edwards Park is in West Price Hill, west of Mount Echo Park. Its extremely plain open shelter is shown in this photograph from 1960. By this time, as in the pavilion at Bellevue Hill Park, concrete had become the primary building material, with brick providing only an accent in the panels between openings. This shelter was demolished in the 1990s.

In December 1956, the newly completed park administration building was ready for occupancy. It was located near the northwest corner of Eden Park, not far from the Elsinore Tower. The Baldwin Piano Company structure is in the background at right. The designer was R. Carl Freund, who designed some three-dozen buildings for Cincinnati's parks between 1930 and his death in 1959 at the age of 57.

Viewed from the street side, the park administration building revealed a more complex form than is apparent from the preceding photograph. In its form, materials, and design, it reflected much of what was happening in city park improvements in the 1950s.

The Taft Museum in Lytle Park was constructed in 1820 for Martin Baum. The house was purchased by the Taft family in the 1870s. Charles and Anna Taft spurred public support for the museum with their 1927 offer to donate their home, art collection, and an endowment. The building opened as a museum in 1932. Among its treasures are murals painted in the 1840s by Robert Duncanson, a well-known African American artist of the period.

A 1963 aerial photograph, oriented north-northwest, shows Lytle Park in its heavily developed urban setting (into which surface parking lots were beginning to intrude). The Taft Museum is hidden by trees along the short piece of Pike Street at the right side of the photograph; Lytle Park extends through the two blocks immediately west of the museum. Freeways had begun to alter the face of Cincinnati by this time, with much more to come.

A gift of the Taft family, the 11-foot bronze statue of Abraham Lincoln in Lytle Park was created by sculptor George Grey Barnard and dedicated in 1917. The Taft Museum is visible in the distance of this photograph from the mid-20th century. After its completion, the statue elicited controversy due to its depiction of Lincoln as having huge hands and looking unusually morose. Today it is widely appreciated as an important work of art.

The original plan of the 1960s proposed running the Northeast Expressway (Interstate Route 71) through Lytle Park. With support of the public and of city councilman Charles Taft II, agreement was reached that at the expense of the Western-Southern Life Insurance Company, the freeway would be "capped" and Lytle Park preserved. This view, dated December 10, 1970, shows the Lincoln statue being reset after the freeway ditch had been capped and park restoration had begun.

Who would guess that Abraham Lincoln today stands above a freeway? This eastward view in 1972 shows the L shape that Lytle Park took due to the freeway project, its area having increased to just over 2 acres. The Taft Museum still crowns the park's east end, with the slopes of Mount Adams visible through the summer haze beyond the museum.

An abstract sculpture rests on one of the islands along Central Parkway. Its French creator, sculptor Jean Boutellis, gave it the title *Aggravation de l'Espace* (Aggravation of Space). Originally located in front of city hall, the sculpture apparently was so annoying to pedestrians that it was moved to this site.

In April 1960, this was the scene along East Second Street in the Yeatman's Cove area of the Cincinnati riverfront. As important as the Ohio River was to the city, it had always been a "working" river, at least along the portion that passed the central part of the city. There were few, if any, opportunities to enjoy the river for recreation, with railroads, warehouses, and industries occupying the land at the water's edge.

In 1962, a park called Yeatman's Cove was built on the river between Broadway and Sycamore Street but was removed in the late 1960s for construction of Riverfront Stadium. A second Yeatman's Cove was completed just upriver from the first in 1976. These projects, along with the construction of Riverfront Stadium, Riverfront Coliseum, and other projects, largely removed the old warehouses and commercial buildings along the river. Yeatman's Cove is managed by the Cincinnati Recreation Commission.

This aerial photograph, taken after 1975 and oriented with south at the top, shows the old Central Bridge and the coliseum at the right. To the left of the bridge is Yeatman's Cove, and directly south of it is Lytle Park. The lanes of Interstate Route 71 come out from under the southwest edge of the park. The Abraham Lincoln statue is in the center of the smaller of the two plazas, with the Taft Museum squeezed between larger buildings at the left edge of the photograph.

A northward view from Newport, Kentucky, shows the Cincinnati skyline of some three decades ago. The then-new stadium and coliseum fill the foreground, with the city core between them dominated by the Central Trust and Carew towers. Boats still tie up at the public landing, keeping the Ohio River a part of life in Cincinnati. Ongoing development of riverfront parklands today will only strengthen that link.

Regardless of the era, any place with a good climbing tree—in this case a sycamore in one of Cincinnati's parks—is a good place for kids. Unstructured playtime is an essential part of growing up; it is obvious that these young people have already learned the benefits of cooperative effort.

There also is a time for structured activity. It is not certain what lessons these youngsters are learning, but most of them seem to be attentive. In the archives of the park board, one can find hundreds of photographs like this of Cincinnatians enjoying one of the nation's premier park systems.

This photograph was probably taken about 1957 or 1958, according to an inscription on the back, on "the warmest December day in 81 years." Why not, then, go to Ault Park for a picnic? The three younger children are absorbed in their meals, while the boy at left is on the verge of digging into his. It's hard to say why his companion across the table looks so glum.

In much more casual dress than would have been typical a half-century earlier, a crowd around the Eden Park Music Pavilion enjoys a concert during warm weather in 1953. The long tradition of free public concerts here and in other city parks is only one of the many benefits Cincinnati's parks have offered over the course of nearly two centuries.

Eden Park still provides dramatic views across the diverse urban landscape of Cincinnati. Beyond the rooftops and chimneys of homes on Mount Adams, this scene encompasses the music hall, at left, and, at center, Cincinnati Union Terminal (today the Cincinnati Museum Center) in the West End neighborhood. The Over-the-Rhine neighborhood sits in front and to the right of the music hall. (Author's collection.)

Six

Cincinnati's Parks Today

The Cincinnati park system today has five regional parks, 70 neighborhood parks, 34 preserves and natural areas, five nature centers, five parkways, 18 scenic overlooks, and 65 miles of hiking and bridle trails. More than 5,000 acres of land make up the system.

Building on the 1992 master plan, the park board has published the Cincinnati Parks 2007 Centennial Master Plan in recognition of the 100 years that have passed since George Kessler's brilliant original plan. Cincinnati can be proud of having implemented that plan, perhaps not entirely in the specific ways Kessler sought, but certainly in ways that met the spirit and the intent of his plan.

To build on an already great park system, the current plan calls for new bike trails, greenways, an expanded parkway system, preservation of river and stream corridors and hillsides, and improvements to neighborhood and regional parks. It urges concentration of these efforts in the core of the city as people have made the decision to live more centrally.

A currently ongoing effort is development of a downtown riverfront park to build on the earlier efforts at Yeatman's Cove and Sawyer Point. This will help accomplish the longterm goal of opening the riverfront for recreational uses that have not been possible for much of Cincinnati's history.

The photographs in this chapter are just a sampling of what awaits visitors to Cincinnati's parks. Each park is distinctive and offers a unique experience. From hiking to historic architecture, from nature studies to outdoor sculpture, these are the places that have made Cincinnati a "city within a park."

The pergola at Alms Park has a stunning view of the Ohio River and the hills of Kentucky. A soft spring day is an ideal time to visit Cincinnati's parks and enjoy such scenes. (Lisa Schafer, Cincinnati Park Board.)

In a look back into the park from the pergola, one of the arches frames the Alms Park Pavilion. The 1929 building has been carefully restored as part of the park system's ongoing program to manage all of its properties so they will continue to serve visitors well into the future. (Author's collection.)

The Alms Park Pavilion today looks as it did when it was erected more than 80 years ago. The arched openings, tile roof, and low wings were inspired by buildings of Renaissance-era Italy. Northeast of this pavilion is a stone cellar where Nicholas Longworth kept the wine produced from the grapes he grew on this land. (Lisa Schafer, Cincinnati Park Board.)

Contrasting with the sophisticated appearance of the pavilion, this Alms Park comfort station is unusual and whimsical. It looks like a leftover medieval fortress, with its massive stone walls and small windows. Its function is more prosaic: a women's room on the top floor and a men's room below. (Author's collection.)

By 1982, the Ault Park Pavilion had deteriorated to such an extent that it was closed to the public. The grand stone steps, too, were in a sorry state, having suffered damage from both vandals and the weather.

Happily, the Ault Park Pavilion was fully restored within a few years and won a state historic preservation award in 1992. The work included restoration of the terrace, gardens, and stepped fountain, all of which were designed by Cleveland landscape architect Albert D. Taylor. (Author's collection.)

A closer view of the pavilion in Ault Park reveals its high level of architectural detail, including both the traditional rough stone found in many of Cincinnati's park buildings, and the cut stone used in the arches, cornices, and balustrades. (Author's collection.)

A 1977 donation by Mrs. Arthur M. Bettman created the Bettman Preserve, a wooded enclave set back on Beech Lane in East Walnut Hills. In the former Bettman home is the Bettman Natural Resource Center, which houses the park board's nature education offices. The board's library and archives also are located here. The sensory garden near the house has concrete paths with raised curbs and overlooks so that people in wheelchairs and the visually impaired can enjoy the trees, shrubs, raised planting beds, light, shade, and sounds of the surrounding woods. (Lisa Schafer, Cincinnati Park Board.)

A few miles west of Alms and Ault Parks atop Mount Adams is Eden Park, considered by many to be the jewel in the crown of the Cincinnati park system. Certainly it is unmatched in the scope and variety of its offerings. One of its most enduring landmarks is the water tower. Here a close-up photograph of the tower's upper levels reveals its high level of architectural detail. (Author's collection.)

One of the original purposes of Eden Park was to contain the city's water supply in a large reservoir. Today a fragment of the stone wall that held back the water remains as an elegant ruin. The former reservoir bottom today is a grassy lawn. (Author's collection.)

When the Eden Park Reservoir was in use, park visitors could walk atop its stone wall to gaze over the water or get a view of Mount Adams. That experience is possible today, permitting a close-up view of the carved stonework and the iron fencing that kept curious park patrons safe. (Author's collection.)

South of the Eden Park Water Tower is the Presidential Grove, established in 1882 when the American Forestry Conference held its first national congress in Cincinnati. A tree has been planted here in honor of each of the presidents of the United States. Broad walkways like these make it easy for all visitors to enjoy this part of the park. (Lisa Schafer, Cincinnati Park Board.)

The chamber of commerce eagles, the stone retaining wall, and the Melan Arch Bridge still stand today in Eden Park, just as they did nearly a century ago. When this view is compared to earlier photographs, the biggest apparent change is in the amount of tree cover. This view looks north toward the south side of the bridge. (Author's collection.)

Down Eden Park Drive and around a curve to the right from the Melan Arch Bridge, the Spring House Gazebo is several years into its second century. It is in excellent condition, a tribute to the care with which the park board has rehabilitated and maintained the dozens of historical structures in the park system. (Author's collection.)

The Eden Park Overlook is behind the Krohn Conservatory and offers one of the spectacular views of the Ohio River Valley that are found in several of Cincinnati's parks. In 1929, Pres. Herbert Hoover dedicated the granite obelisk here to observe completion of the lock-and-dam system that made the Ohio River into a steady and reliable transportation artery. (Author's collection.)

In a quieter and more secluded area of Eden Park, the 1903 concrete bridge spans the narrow neck of water that connects the Twin Lakes. This part of the park was renovated in the 1990s. (Author's collection.)

At the end of a path near the west end of the concrete bridge, a gift from Gifu, Japan, a sister city of Cincinnati, depicts the practice of fishing with birds rather than nets or poles. Beginning in medieval times, Japanese fishermen used cormorants, a fish-eating seabird that dove underwater to catch fish. Men and their birds worked at night, using torches to attract the fish. A long cord and a metal ring around the cormorants' necks enabled the fishermen to retrieve each bird after it caught a fish; the metal ring kept the birds from swallowing the fish, which the fishermen forced the birds to disgorge. This practice endures today in some areas of Japan and has been immortalized in Cincinnati by this distinctive sculpture. (Both photographs, author's collection.)

The sculpture *Capitoline Wolf* replicates an ancient statue on one of the seven hills of Rome. The sculpture represents the legend of Romulus and Remus, who as infants were suckled by a she-wolf and as adults founded the Eternal City. The Eden Park statue was dedicated in 1932 as a gift from the City of Rome to honor the general Cincinnatus, the inspiration for the Queen City's name (see page 127). (Author's collection.)

A grove of trees in Eden Park shelters the Seasongood Pavilion, a bandstand that continues the long tradition of hosting musical performances in the park. The structure, dedicated in 1960, was the gift of Martha S. Stern to commemorate her brother Murray Seasongood's service as mayor of the city. Concrete terraces supporting the bench seats are porous, allowing rainwater to soak into the soil and reducing runoff. (Lisa Schafer, Cincinnati Park Board.)

On the lawn next to the entrance drive to the Cincinnati Art Museum rests a 10-ton steel sculpture titled *Atman*. Standing 32 feet high and bright red in color, it is hard to miss as one passes through Eden Park. It was installed in 1986, the work of sculptor Mark Di Suvero. He was born in Shanghai, and the sculpture's title means "World Soul." (Author's collection.)

The Vietnam Veterans Memorial in Eden Park was dedicated in 1984 and depicts one white and one African American soldier, symbolic of all who served in that controversial conflict between 1959 and 1975. The pink granite base includes an incised map of the two Vietnams, North and South, marked with their respective capitals and with the demilitarized zone that separated them. (Author's collection.)

Cincinnati's first African American mayor (1972–1975) is commemorated in the Theodore M. Berry International Friendship Park, which occupies 20 acres along the eastern riverfront area. The park is below Mount Adams and east of the Interstate Route 471 bridge. The park opened in May 2003 and features winding walkways, a pavilion, an international plaza with ceremonial flags, sculptures, a serpentine sitting wall, and gardens representing the earth's continents. (Lisa Schafer, Cincinnati Park Board.)

At one location in Burnet Woods, visitors have a choice of how to navigate a change in elevation—standing up or sitting down. The well-polished appearance of the slide suggests that many people (presumably mostly kids, but certainly some adults as well) have taken the latter option. (Author's collection.)

Lytle Park at the east end of downtown is still identified by one of the historical bronze signs that can be found in a few of the city's parks. The wording in the upper and lower borders reads "Park Board, City of Cincinnati." The ornamented border and the fluted column suggest the care and thought that was typical of the design of park improvements in the early 20th century. (Author's collection.)

The pavilion at Inwood Park still has the hip roof it received in 1913 (see pages 57 and 58), although the original ceramic tile surface has given way to modern shingles. Otherwise it is little changed. Were the children who stood in one of its doorways so long ago (see page 72) to visit today, they certainly would recognize it. (Author's collection.)

The shelter in Daniel Drake Park dates from 1957. The park is located in Kennedy Heights on the west side of Interstate Route 71. Drake was a naturalist and physician and was founder of the city's first medical college. The shelter is a little unusual, featuring a large and high gable roof. It also has the rough stone walls and pillars so prevalent in the architecture of Cincinnati's park system. (Author's collection.)

The Mount Echo Pavilion, at an elevation of some 300 feet above the Ohio River, provides unmatched vistas, even on a rainy day. Mount Echo Park also still has its massive stone retaining wall at the entrance (see pages 62 and 63), looking much as it did when completed nearly 100 years ago. (Author's collection.)

Thornton Triangle in the Sayler Park area is among the smallest parks in Cincinnati. Eliza Thornton erected this monument there in 1912 in memory of her architect husband, J. Fitzhugh Thornton. After being damaged by a car in 1940, the statue was sold. Angry citizens demanded its return. In time it was found, repurchased, and returned to its rightful location in 1941. It has been repaired and recast. (Author's collection.)

Piatt Park, considered Cincinnati's original park, still welcomes downtown lunchtime crowds (see pages 16 and 17), although this morning view was taken before the daily crowd arrived. The seat walls are recent, and the park offers free Internet access. (Lisa Schafer, Cincinnati Park Board.)

Seasongood Square in North Avondale has one of the park system's more unusual buildings, a round comfort station with a conical roof. It dates from 1930 and has a stucco exterior, distinguishing it from the system's other round comfort station, which was built of rough stone in Alms Park (see page 109) in 1936. R. Carl Freund, a prolific architect park architect for 25 years, designed both. (Author's collection.)

The Colerain Avenue waiting station at the main entrance to Mount Airy Forest today looks much more finished than it did in the view on page 90. Mount Airy Forest is the largest city park by far and offers perhaps the most thorough wilderness experience of all the parks. Even the presence of steady traffic cutting through the middle of the park on Interstate Route 74 does not spoil the experience. (Author's collection.)

Miles of trails and steep topography make Mount Airy Forest a challenge for hikers. Fortunately, well-planned steps and bridges designed to fit into the forest setting help to ease the journey. (Author's collection.)

For those seeking a somewhat tamer version of the outdoor experience, the Mount Airy Arboretum might provide the answer. The arboretum building, designed by R. Carl Freund, was completed in 1953. This photograph looks over one of the nearby landscaped hillsides. (Author's collection.)

One of the open shelters in Mount Airy Forest is a good example of the park rustic design used for many of these structures. Debarked tree trunks and limbs were used as columns, beams, rafters, and other structural elements, while rough stone pillars and walls completed the composition. (Author's collection.)

The Tree House is one of the more recent structures in Mount Airy Forest. Ingeniously designed to be completely accessible, the whimsical building, in which there seem to be very few right angles, wraps itself around trees and sits high above the ground. It has wood siding but otherwise is designed much the way the park rustic shelters and pavilions were designed many decades ago. (Author's collection.)

The Tree House's debt to earlier park building designs is apparent once a visitor steps inside. A creative blend of rough and saw-cut wood gives the building a unique feel while still giving it a character that blends well with its woodland setting. (Author's collection.)

Out in the woods of Mount Airy Forest, a visitor can find his way around using an old-fashioned version of GPS ("Go Peer at a Sign," perhaps?) rather than today's electronic gadgets. Maybe that is what parks are for, after all—to spend some time away from the material goods and distractions of modern life. (Author's collection.)

The story of Cincinnatus tells of a Roman aristocrat of the fifth century BCE who was forced to give up his lands and property to pay a heavy fine for his son's misdeeds. The father then lived humbly on a small farm until he was called to serve as the Roman dictator when the city was threatened by hostile tribes. After defeating these enemies, Lucius Quinctius Cincinnatus gave up power. Early in American history, George Washington emulated Cincinnatus by giving up the almost absolute power he held during the Revolutionary War. The Society of the Cincinnati, the inspiration for the Queen City's name, was formed at that time to honor men who followed these examples of virtuous leadership and service to country. In these photographs of the Cincinnati Recreation Commission's Bicentennial Commons at Sawyer Point, Cincinnati's namesake stands by his plow, ready to return to the life of a farmer as he gives up the fasces, the traditional symbol of power in ancient Rome. However, Cincinnatus has further vicissitudes to endure in the form of the occasional Ohio River flood.

Consistent with our mission to preserve history on a local level, this book was printed in South Carolina on American-made paper and manufactured entirely in the United States. Products carrying the accredited Forest Stewardship Council (FSC) label are printed on 100 percent FSC-certified paper.

MADE IN THE USA